Theories and Equipment For The Paranormal Hobbyist

Edward W. Krietemeyer

DEDICATION

To my cat Oscar, who takes an interest in me only at feeding time!

.

CONTENTS

ACKNOWLEDGMENTS

Co-founder STEVE WATSON
Photographer CANDY RIGGS
Researcher FRANK ANDERSON
Researcher DON STOCUM

ABOUT THE AUTHOR

Edward W. Krietemeyer had his first experience with the supernatural at the age of five with the death of his grandmother. Nothing was further from his mind when he had his second experience 30 years later with a haunting in a home he previously owned. He was determined to know how and why these things occurred, and started exploring the unknown to gathered evidence to better understand his experience. Was it real, or a trick of the mind? This book answers most of the questions for the beginner in the paranormal field. If you are just interested in exploring the paranormal, wanting to join a paranormal team, or just curious about the paranormal field.

Easy to build equipment that will save hundreds of dollars if you were to buy them online. What equipment do you really need to start with? What should I know about the paranormal before I begin? Written and priced with the paranormal hobbyist in mind.

INTRODUCTION

There is a lengthy process involved before any observation can become a theory. The event must be witnessed multiple times, so that basic guidelines and methods are created to arrive at a more practical means of measurement, and documentation. Many more questions, and observations are made before forming the first of many hypotheses. The hypothesis is nothing more than an educated guess that must have a basic understanding of what is being observed, and form testable predictions. Most early hypotheses are usually wrong and in science, that is a part of the self-correcting function of the scientific method. Having a working hypothesis for what has been up to that point, a never seen before event, or occurrence is rare. Hypotheses are the first in many steps in the learning process. When the hypothesis overtime has shown testable consistency in its predictions then it becomes a theory. Even then, new experiments can yield new results causing a rethink of the original hypothesis, corrections, or throwing out the theory all together in light of a newer theory that best meets the observation. Remember there are always those first couple of steps we should never accept any hypothesis or theory without mountains of evidence and lots of scrutiny. After a theory has withstood the test of time it then becomes a law such as Newton's laws of gravity, and motion, but even Sir Isaac Newton, the greatest scientist of his time made mistakes. There is nothing absolute when it comes to knowledge realistically we are always just one next best guess away. In the paranormal field theories abound based on no real research that I can find most of them should be considered more of a concept then an actual theory. In this so-called paranormal field / hobby, any answer is accepted as fact even though it has been proven repeatedly to be wrong, and baseless just for the sake of believing. In this book, I will put forth many old and new ideas in the method of thinking outside of the box to come up with ways to test these ideas making sitting around in the dark a little more practical.

The stigma of being labeled a pseudoscience incites the subject of ghosts, or haunted houses as a topic of humor. It is understandable why many professionals would avoid anything labeled pseudoscience for fear that it would tarnish a struggling reputation, and limit career opportunities.

Unfortunately, there are many frauds, and the falsifying of data for the purpose of notoriety, but the same thing is true for mainstream science. Most researchers believe in legitimate research with falsifiable results. In real science, scrutiny comes from educated professionals through a complex process of peer review. Skepticism is replaced with a collection of constructive alternatives. There is a promising study underway called "The Human Consciousness Project" which is the collaboration of independent researchers, medical centers, and colleges throughout the world. As medical science explores the complexity of the human mind, and looks to explain the nature of human consciousness. "The most intriguing aspect of the study is its attempt to study consciousness during clinical death. That our human mind and consciousness may in fact constitute a separate undiscovered entity apart from the brain. The implications not only for science, but also for all of humanity." If we discover that, our consciousness can survive death. This would inevitably result in a new chapter in medical science, but would ultimately create more questions than answers. I hold out a lot of hope that this project will uncover some part of our human consciousness that can explain what serious researchers and I have already observed first hand.

Theories and research is the lifeblood of science and it all starts with an observation followed by a question. I have assembled many of the known paranormal theories from early in the field of parapsychology from the 1960s to some lesser-known theories and some of my own that I have revised from my early years in paranormal research. I have no idea who originally came up with most of them I have added the names to the ones I can fine who originated them. All of these theories including mine are merely guesses based on observations. Some of these theories have been passed around true or not for decades taken entirely on belief.

PARANORMAL THEORIES: CONSCIOUS ENERGY

By Edward Krietemeyer

There has been a growing interest in the concept of the mind as a conscious form of energy. Parapsychologists have long since studied physical energy and how it can be triggered by thought. Laboratory tests demonstrate that a weak coupling between physical energy and a sort of human "magnetic field" around the body that can move or influence objects. Neurologists divide memory into long-term and short-term memory. Our short-term memory is believed to be formed by brief changes in synaptic plasticity transmissions, or by a type of reverberating feedback circuit, where a memory is held bio-electrically within a loop, and is the brain's mechanism for remembering information in use.

The research of Dr. Celia Green of the Institute of Psychophysical Research found that 12% of single (OBE) cases occurred during sleep, 32% when unconscious, and 25% were associated with some kind of psychological stress, such as worry, extreme fatigue, or fear. Such as the extreme fear that would accompany physical trauma. (i.e. Death)

In 1968, Dr. Green published an analysis of 400 first-hand accounts of out-of-body experiences. This represented the first attempt to provide taxonomy of such experiences once viewed as simply anomalous perceptual experiences, or hallucinations.

In this theory, we are focusing specifically on the kind of energy that is associated with consciousness, our brains higher-level biophysical energy. In the case of out-of-body experiences, the consciousness seems to depart the body for brief periods, enabling observation of the world from a point of view other than that of the one's own physical body. This usually occurs under trauma, or extreme stress. For example, when one's heart stops beating momentarily, the shock of the event could cause an out-of-body experience. You could be a witness to your own death, or falling from a great height, realizing that death is imminent. At the moment of death, the link is broken. Without a host to feed your consciousness, you would be drawn to other energy sources. Conscious Energy would be strongly attracted to you because of its familiarity with the human life force or physical energy. Our bodies naturally produce a subtle magnetic field, so it would only be practical to assume that conscious energy would be drawn to a familiar source to feed it.

Physical Energy

Through a biochemical process, our body naturally generates 10 to 100 mV of electricity and a subtle magnetic field. According to electromagnetic theory, any current flowing through a conductor will produce a magnetic field. This is true in the human body as electrical signals are conducted through neurons and muscles. The electrical energy our body generates is between 250–900 kilovolts daily and is produced from the process of metabolizing "food" and "oxygen." On average, our body produces as much thermal (body heat) energy daily as a 100-watt light bulb measured as direct current DC.

A human body can generate between 10 and 100 millivolts
Human Body 62-78 MHz DC – Direct Current

The human brain uses around 20 Watts of it.
Normal Brain Frequency 72 MHz
Frequency range of the Brain is between 0.5Hz and 50Hz

There are naturally occurring minerals that also produce magnetic fields, and can sustain magnetic patterns. High concentrations of these minerals such as limestone used in wall plaster up to the mid twentieth century, and has been cited as the cause of a recurring form of paranormal event known as a Residual Haunt. We believed that the entity that is created by use of this method is nothing more than an electromagnetic pattern, a snapshot of our bioelectrical memory process at the point of death. Later experiments done by the team will show a more complex consciousness is involved including a full range of our higher-level cognition. The capability of learning beyond the time of its creation has been validated repeatedly of the course of seven years of research. It carries on as a remnant of a once-living human being. It is limited in its knowledge to the era in which it lived.

Hypothesis

If our bioelectrical consciousness has the ability to extend outside of its physical host induce by trauma. First identified in 1968 from the case studies of Dr. Celia Green that associated some types of psychological stress, extreme fear, and physical trauma caused by death itself triggering an Out of Body Experience - OBE. Then death would be the method of breaking the connection to our physical host. Our conscious-self would exist by imprinting, or anchoring itself to a suitable substrate, feeding off the physical, or any artificial energy source producing an electromagnetic field in a limited existence, nothing more than a parasite. Manipulating its electromagnetic properties to influence the physical world. This would explain mood swings, and physical weakness, and why some activity is stronger at some locations compared to others.

Inducing an Out-of-Body - OBE Event

This test was designed to induce trauma through a level of stress that would be present as our conscious self was faced with death. This is a more radical method to trigger the out-of-body experience than methods, such as meditation. The process leading up to the event is designed to weaken the body and to fatigue and stress the mind. The test subject is informed of a white card that will be used to validate the event. A word will be written at the time, just before triggering the event. The test subject is informed that once the OBE is triggered, they must read the word on the card. The card will be introduced in the test environment on a stand facing away from the test subject and will only be known by the test coordinator. When testing ends, the coordinator or pre-designated official will remove and seal the card in an envelope that will be placed in a locked container such as a bank safe- deposit box, or an equally secure location until the test subject recovers. However, the details of how to test this theory will not be published in this book do to physical and mental health concerns to individuals that would attempt to induce an OBE.

Observation

How can entities pull off such complicated procedures without shown cognitive ability or having a physical presents. It is beyond reason that the entity would have powers and abilities beyond its once human state. My team and I has personally felt, heard, saw, recorded, and experienced paranormal activity with undeniable human characteristics. The question is can you say without a doubt if it is the effect of a Ghost, and that is really the bottom line. It always comes down to that one question. Therefore, I believe the question itself needs more scrutiny. Let us first start looking at the origins, and how the word was used throughout history, and its original meaning to come to a more factual understanding of what a Ghost originally implied. Remember the public has been inundated for some time with reality TV shows with Ghost Hunting, can I call them enthusiast? That runs up, and down hallways trying to capture Ghosts! A Ghost is unlike the word Spirit that is described as a non-corporeal substance, is the manifestation of the spirit itself. The word Ghost came from the Hebrew, and old English translation of the word "gast" that originally meant stranger, or foreigner. Throughout recorded human history, you could say the civilization itself would not exist if it were not for the realization that there is a human spirit that carries on after death. The pyramids, and early Neolithic structures even religion itself proves that spirit activity exists, and has always existed. It has been only until now that we are on the fringes of technology that can physically prove it with data logging equipment backed by video, and audio. Our research in this field has concluded that it is not Spirit, or Ghost as based on earlier definitions. It is more than that, a type of human consciousness that on extremely rare and very limited conditions exist as a normal part of our everyday lives. Others have defined a ghost being a form of disembodied conscious energy. Energy itself cannot be free flowing for energy to exist in any state it would have to be attached to something that feeds it. Energy cannot exist in a self-sustaining state. New research from Physicists at Cuza University in Romania was the first to create a new life form from gaseous plasma. These are "cells" with a boundary made up of two layers an outer layer of negatively charged electrons and an inner layer of positively charged ions. Trapped inside the boundary they discovered an inner nucleus of gas atoms. These "cells" met criteria for life: the ability to replicate, to communicate information, and to metabolize and grow. They could not be considered alive because of lack of inherited material. However, this discovery may hint at a drastic re-think of what is necessary for life, and opens the door on the possibility of other forms of life far beyond what had previously been accepted.

We know there is some kind of limited existence that mimics the characteristics of a living human being. Serious researchers over the past decade have collected overwhelming data that would be described as a type of disembodied consciousness. The next step is for medical science to announce what has already been known since the dawn of human civilization.

QUANTUM BRAIN THEORY

By Dr. Hammeroff, and Physicist Sir Roger Penrose

Put forth a new theory in Consciousness, biology and quantum hypotheses: Inside each brain cell, there are fibrous called microtubules, hollow rods that function primarily to help support and shape the cell. Quantum processes called entanglement is believed to play a pivotal role in human consciousness. Quantum effects have been shown to control several biological processes, and when the microtubules die, they lose their quantum state. The quantum information cannot be destroyed it can instead redistribute into our surroundings. Quantum effects can continue outside the body and can exists indefinitely.

STRUCTURAL COHESION

By Edward Krietemeyer
(Entities Strength)

Conscious Energy states that the entity is the electromagnetic pattern of a once living human being, and is the bases upon how the entity can use its electromagnetic properties to manipulate its environment. The strength of the entity is in the structural cohesion, or binding of its pattern. The denser the electromagnetic pattern the stronger the entity, and the greater the activity. To inhibit the electromagnetic binding or cohesiveness of the pattern could theoretically end the haunt.

This can be done in many ways.

1. Enhancing the ground: This would create barriers but would not end the haunt.
2. Low level electromagnetic pulse: This would degrade the entities electromagnetic pattern without structural cohesion within the pattern the entity ceases to exist. A strong enough pulse would rid any imprinted objects of the pattern, corrupting the pattern.

Sunlight generally and in the most basic of terms has a scattering effect on electromagnetic waves, so the structural cohesiveness. Alternatively, electromagnetic binding of the entities pattern would be weakening during the day. Denser structures that are shielded from the effects of the sun such as lower levels sub-structures, a basement for instance. Would also explain why activity is predominantly greater in such locations. Seasonal and atmospheric changes can all aid in the strength of the entity. In the early morning, an hour just before dawn, and late afternoon as the radiation from the Sun is slowly diffuse. The lowest point in this cycle is between 2 to 4 AM, which could answer the question of why activity is stronger at night then during the day.

Revised: To date there is no proof that the entity can manipulate the electromagnetic field, or that they exist as all. Event thought the activities that are generally associated with ghost are common. We still do not know why or how they exist, or speak, eye, move objects without a physical presence. Even if one-day medical science proves that human consciousness can survive death there is still linking the activities of ghost to a once living human being.

Impression Theory

Ghosts might not be the spirit of the dead, but an impression of the presence of the living. Our existence affects our environment around us perception dictates our reality. I have always wondered is the ghost a once living human being that we believe it is, or a representation of our very presence that is reflected back to us. Is that what we call a ghost merely the reflection of emotions caused by the living? This has more to do with the physical and mental state that our beliefs are so strong that it clouds our judgment from what we want to fine to what we found could only be described as a ghost.

Thoughts: This is one of the pit falls in science wanting it to be very so bad that we accept it as real even with all its flaws. This is why peer review is so important its self-correcting process that points out problems and suggesting corrections or throwing it out altogether. What is believed to be true today may not be tomorrow. If there is anything we can depend on, it is change.

DIMENSIONAL CONSCIOUSNESS

"A ghost is a human being who has passed out of the physical body, usually in a traumatic state and is not aware usually of his true condition. We are all spirits encased in a physical body. At the time of passing, our spirit body continues into the next dimension. A ghost, on the other hand, due to trauma, is stuck in our physical world and needs to be released to go on."
~ Dr. Hans Holzer

Fourth Dimensional Consciousness
By Edward Krietemeyer

Energy should be able to pass through the dimensions. The fourth dimension over laps the third if a three dimensional being can cast a two dimensional shadow then a fourth dimensional being can cast a three dimensional shadow. If a three dimensional shadow of a fourth dimensional being passed through our three dimensional plain of existence. The appearance would seem to fade in and out as it passes through solid structures, only to dissipate as it crosses between our three dimensional perimeters. The full-bodied apparition that was caught on video had such details as a head, arms, legs, and you could even make out the period clothing it wore. We believe the apparition is a projection of how the entity last perceived itself. It faded into view with an almost milky white appearance, and looked solid before walking through a table then faded away. A fourth dimensional theory comes closest to explaining what was observed. We are still no closer in figuring out what it truly is.

If our consciousness can transcend the dimensions, then what we are observing could be nothing more than shadows of a fourth dimensional existence. My team has worked on ways to validate this theory. In our dimensional experiment, we would be setting up multiple simultaneous experiments. The focus would be on conducting an EVP session of a deceased individual at multiple locations in the individual's life: where they died, where they lived, where they were laid to rest. Each team would be given a list of identical questions. Each question would be asked **simultaneously** at a predetermined time.

We planned this experiment at a known haunt. Where over the past year from 2010 through 2011 has had an ongoing dialog with an entity that was very consistent with its responses. We wanted to know what state of being the entity was in. Through our research, we have determined that there are only two logical possibilities. Three Dimensional State such as the one we exist in now, or a Fourth Dimensional Being?

The fourth dimension is the only other dimension that can cross through our three dimensional plane of existence. Four-dimensional space can cast a three dimensional image, or a shadow of itself. The eye and a camera can perceive a three dimensional image. The camera can capture that image, and render it as a two dimensional photograph. Three-dimensional shadows could explain sighting of full-bodied apparitions.

How to test a Dimensional Theory

If the description of a four-dimensional being is correct, the entity can take up multiple three-dimensional planes of space. Then to test this theory we would need to ask simultaneous question in multiple areas of the location. By reviewing, the audio for simultaneous responses would point to a four-dimensional state of being. Individual responses would point to a three-dimensional existence as in the one we are in.

THE TIME SLIP THEORY (TIME TRAVEL)

"In his memoirs, Einstein wrote that he was disturbed that his equations contained solutions that allowed for time travel. However, he finally concluded: the universe does not rotate, it expands (i.e. as in the Big Bang theory) and hence Goedel's solution could be thrown out for "physical reasons." (Apparently, if the Big Bang was rotating, then time travel would be possible throughout the universe!)"

There is the belief that time is the fourth dimension. That we can slip through into different points in the past and future. This works from the premise that time is fluid rather than fixed. Time is not linear as we experience it, but exists within a context of a single point of space. If true, it is not hard to believe a person could slip from one point in time to another. Kind of the way we in our normal day would move from one room to another in our house. As such, the image of an apparently very solid personality moving through a mansion completely oblivious to the presence of the observer may not be paranormal, but a snapshot from an earlier time that somehow played to the observer. This could explain ghost that are residual haunts or manifestation. Residual is where the spirit does the same thing every time it is seen or heard. It is like a film just playing repeatedly. Are they just oblivious to our world not cause there dead but cause they somehow stepped out of time? How this could happen is still not known but could explain how ordinary rational people reported being surrounded by ancient time's for minute's even hours.

Thoughts: According to String, theory elementary particles rise from the different quantum states of these strings containing eleven-dimensions or more called M-theory and are the only candidate for a complete theory of the universe. Many physicists and mathematicians have postulated that the fourth dimension exists and that we could exist within the shadow of a greater fourth dimensional world. Weather time is the fourth or the eleventh many physicists believe time travel is possible.

THERMAL COMPRESSION

By Edward Krietemeyer

When applying electromagnetic forces to control the motion of the surrounding molecules through acting upon their orbital electrons in the atoms of each molecule, and by having corresponding electromagnetic fields intersecting in the direction of motion bunches up and collides with the other air molecules. By repeating this process in rapid succession, it may be possible to agitate enough molecules to alter the state of the atmosphere at the conversion point. Energy being transferred from molecule to molecule is exchanged and the balance of charge is altered. In the field, paranormal researchers observe rapid fluctuations in temperature where heat is generated and then dissipated rapidly. In Maxwell's Theory, this would create the super cooling effect as the molecules returned to their abeyance state. This anomaly would appear to change its mass and or weight at the conversion point. The weight at the conversion point combined with motion could be used as force against objects. Thermal Compression Theory is the attempt to explain hot and cold spots observed during paranormal activity.

Maxwell's Theory

Although air molecules are invisible, they still have weight and take up space. There are 2.7×10^{19} (approximately 30,000,000,000,000,000,000) molecules in every cubic centimeter of air. When you compress air, it heats up because the molecules in it are excited; when you decompress air, it cools down. If you were to take the heated compressed air and then allow the heat to dissipate before decompressing it, the cooling caused by the decompression will drop the temperature of the gas below its condensation point.

Hypothesis

When applying electromagnetic forces to control the motion of the surrounding molecules through acting upon their orbital electrons in the atoms of each molecule, and by having corresponding electromagnetic fields intersecting in the direction of motion bunches up and collides with the other air molecules. By repeating this process in rapid succession, it may be possible to agitate enough molecules to alter the state of the atmosphere at the conversion point. Energy being transferred from molecule to molecule is exchanged and the balance of charge is altered. In the field, paranormal researchers observe rapid fluctuations in temperature where heat is generated and then dissipated rapidly. In Maxwell's Theory, this would create the super cooling effect as the molecules returned to their abeyance state. This anomaly would appear to change its mass and or weight at the conversion point. The weight at the conversion point combined with motion could be used as force against objects. This would explain why objects that have been moved have been reported being cold to the touch.

Thoughts: To date there has been no proof that the entity is capable of such a complex and scientifically impossible process. Nor would it be able to create enough pressure or mass to move objects some of excess of 80 pounds, which is the heaviest, documented weight ever moved entirely on its own.

Cold Spot Theory: It is believed that an entity can draw the thermal energy out of the air in order to manifest itself there for creating the cold spot.

Thoughts: There is no correlation between temperature changes and the activities of ghosts.

ACOUSTICAL ENERGY

By Edward Krietemeyer

As human beings, we learn to speak at an early age it is an ingrained part of our conscious self. Our conscious self-projects the sound of our voice. It is the manipulation of electromagnetic frequencies that is the essence of our consciousness, which in turn reproduces patterns of audible sound by resonating nearby objects converting. The electromagnetic frequencies into acoustical energy commonly known as a disembodied voice. In my original theory, I held that the Acoustical Energy created in this manner could produce sound that would envelop the area in which it was being generated. This was known as Omni- Sound Theory, meaning that the sound being generated would come from all directions simultaneously. In later observations it looked as if the sound was being targeted, generating acoustical sound as it impacts at or near its intended target. This idea was based on new technology A Electromagnetic Frequency Sound Transducer (Induction Dynamics Solid Drive) utilizes very high-powered neodymium magnets that operate on very low power. This sound transducer transmits acoustical energy through almost any solid surface, transforming the entire surface-with a frequency response of 60 Hz to 15 kHz into a high-quality sound source.

Revised: This is one of my earliest concepts that describe how a disembodied voice or EVP occurs from the result of manipulation of the electromagnetic spectrum, thus transmitting its low electromagnetic frequencies through a solid surface to produce acoustical or audible sound. Of course, this is wrong although we still do not know how the voice is generated. In fact, we do not know if what we call a ghosts even exist at all.

RESIDUAL HAUNT

By Thomas Charles

"Stone Tape Theory is a paranormal hypothesis that was proposed in the 1970s as a possible explanation for ghosts. It speculates that inanimate materials can absorb some form of energy from living beings; the hypothesis speculates that this 'recording' happens especially during moments of high tension, such as murder, or during intense moments of one's life. This stored energy can be released at any given moment, resulting in a display of the occurred activity. According to this hypothesis, ghosts are not spirits at all, but simply non-interactive recordings, similar to a movie. Thomas Charles was one of the first to promulgate the hypothesis of residual haunting."

Revised: This type of haunt is the second most common haunt besides electronic voice phenomena EVP based on a similar concept of low amplitude acoustical sound.

The anomaly occurred this Residual Haunt daily at 11:45 at the location. Wherein 1974 there was a house fire, no one died, but the trauma of that day is forever imprinted into the property.

Help Me Help Me Daddy snd.sc/10su5Jo

Earlier Imprinting theories encompassed personal objects, belonging to a once- living human being, attaching their life force to the object known as a Residual Haunt. In most cases, the human being imprinted their life force by repeating a routine repeatedly for years on end. We once thought that Residual Haunts were caused when the imprinter died, and the activity continued. What we eventually learned is that trauma can be imprinted in different ways, and there is no need for a death. There is a Residual Haunt in which trauma is imprinted by the victims. In one particular case, children were being abused. The children's fear played out repeatedly in the haunt. The owner of the residence knew the family, and they are all very much alive.

Construction is commonly reported as the cause of new or increased activity. It is not so much that the entity likes or dislikes what you are doing.

In this case, it is the powerful tools and equipment being used which send spikes of EMF through a once-dormant location thus resurrecting the patterns. Another form of imprinting is caused by death itself. When a body dies, the life force energy begins to dissipate, leaving its pattern on that spot. It is similar to a Residual Haunt, except there is nothing being played out. All that is left behind is the static image of a once living human being at the time of death.

Bioelectrical Finger Print - Imprinting Theory

There is this fine line yet to be explored in understanding this category of haunt. That is one of the reasons behind my interest in investigating roadside memorials. Imprinting as in residual activity, ownership, or bonding to an object like a Doll. If someone died in an accident, and then was laid out on the side of the road would they leave a bioelectrical fingerprint on that spot as the body dissipates? The trauma itself would have already occurred in the vehicle at the instance of the fatality. Therefore, we are not really looking for a Ghost, but maybe another category of imprinting, or different type of residual haunt. I believe it is a completely new category of haunt a type of bioelectrical image that could exist.

EVP session was conducted at a roadside memorial in a secluded area. The roadside memorial had names on the two larger crosses. There were two smaller crosses with no names placed in the front facing the side of the road. We picked up humming audibly by both researchers, and both audio recorders as the sound anomaly walked around us.

ELECTRONIC VOICE PHENOMENA

By Konstantin Raudive

Electronic Voice Phenomena Theory: EVP refers to voices that appear on recording devices (such as tape recorders) with no apparent source. Swedish film producer, Friedrich Juergenson, while recording bird song in a forest for an upcoming movie, first discovered the phenomenon. He heard two very faint but audible voices while playing back the recording he had made through a reel-to-reel machine. The first was the voice of a man speaking of the bird song at night, and the other was that of his mother calling him by his nickname and saying he was being watched over.

Electronic voice phenomena are described as being at a range of 60 Hz and lower. Showing up on a wideband spectrogram on average within the range of 1kHz-4kHz, it's not so much that it's above or below the range of human hearing just that the amplitude is too faint to be captured by the human ear. When the volume played back, it is turn all the way up the same goes for audio editors. We found it necessary to use headphone amplifiers in aiding us in identifying the sound anomalies, audio spectrum analysis, and procedures are developed along with training to ask questions that would require an extended answer at the point where we would be listening for the response. An extensive understanding, and comprehensive knowledge of Acoustic and Articulatory Phonetics are requires in separating the differences between noise and human speech patterns from the artificial characteristics of a true EVP. The experiments we have conducted show that the entity exists well within our physical plain of existence.

I have been comparing frequencies of reoccurring clear electronic voice phenomenon from the same entity repeating the same word, each time the same word was repeated at the same frequency. This could suggest that the entity has a unique frequency fingerprint for certain words. The word was her name Roxanna that was recorded on different dates, and times.

Another comparison between three samples of Electronic Voice Phenomena (EVP) of different words from different entities. Again, each EVP is within the human audible range of hearing but are too faint to be captured by the human ear. Another observation is that of targeting in which low electromagnetic frequencies impact at or near the intended surface, the produce localized acoustical energy, resulting in audible sound.

Revised: We have developed techniques and procedures along with the use of software spectrum analysis, and educated ourselves in acoustic and articulatory phonetics to identify, and validate electronic voice phenomena - EVP responses. We have found answers for some of the more skeptical arguments about EVP none of which holds up when comparing RF, and noise contamination to a valid EVP response.

In the midst of darkness: the study of ghosts on Amazon

Evidence collected using the methodology in the field of Articulatory Phonetics that is comprised of the study of the sounds of human speech. Spectrum Analysis is an advanced mathematical technique for the study of frequencies according to its component wavelengths producing a visual representation call a spectrogram, or sonogram. Primarily used in astronomy, music, electronics, and signal research. EVP responses are one of the most well documented observations of unexplained audio phenomenon. Once analyzed in a spectrogram and compared with other documented categorize sound samples. There is not the sliest resemblance between a valid EVP response, and the general skeptical explanation of RF contamination, noise, and breath.

How voice recorders can record what or ears cannot hear. The average frequency ranges on these devises are between 40Hz-21kHz well within the range of human hearing 20Hz-20kHz. Electronic voice phenomena are described as being at a range of 60 Hz and lower. Showing up on a wideband spectrogram on average within the range of 1kHz-4kHz, it's not so much that it's above or below the range of human hearing just that the amplitude is too faint to be captured by the human ear. When the volume played back, it is turn all the way up the same goes for audio editors. We found it necessary to use headphone amplifiers in aiding us in identifying the sound anomalies, audio spectrum analysis, and procedures are developed along with training to ask questions that would require an extended answer at the point where we would be listening for the response. An extensive understanding, and comprehensive knowledge of Acoustic and Articulatory Phonetics are requires in separating the differences between noise and human speech patterns from the artificial characteristics of a true EVP. The experiments we have conducted show that the entity exists well within our physical plain of existence.

There is a University Study published in 2012 of a series of experiments that were carried out in Vigo, Spain throughout a period of two years under conditions controlled to the highest degree achievable titled: "A Two-Year Investigation of the Allegedly Anomalous Electronic Voices or EVP by Corresponding author: Anabela Cardoso" outlined some of the problems we've had with stomach noises, whispering, sound being mistaken for voices, and contamination. Everything we have already addressed, and so did the report. Their conclusion was that it was very and yet unexplained.

We get just as good of evidence during the Day, as well as with the lights on, or off. The big advantage to investigating at night is noise! Since most of the evidence you catch are EVP! Noise of any kind even outside noise, if it can be prevented will save evidence. What do I mean save evidence: Training to keep your voice down and that is everyone? Not to walk on someone is EVP, we wait 15 sec after asking the question in silence relaxing our breathing and even holding our breath for the 15 sec. Tag any unavoidable noise! We use a decibel meter where we train people to speak at a moderate tone around 50-60 dB, we have a saying "Their dead not deaf" No yelling out your questions, No whispering, No playing around when someone is asking questions. Using an external microphone on your voice recorder will eliminate the noise of your fingers touching the recorder. Most likely, the entity you are screaming at is standing right beside you. We know by testing with Zoom 360 microphones that the entity targets its electromagnetic voice. We have laid out voice recorders in circles, end to end, side to side, directly in front of the researchers. We found the entity targets its response. In one experiment when we looked at the audio from the Zoom 360 microphones, it showed a linear path across the room to the researcher's recorder, and the response was only on that recorder. We have setup the team around a table with their recorders in front of them showing targeted responses. Experimentation is a part of the scientific methods I listed earlier.

While listening to the recording, you should note if the background noise appears to fade drastically when a real, loud sound is picked up. This means that your recorder probably has an auto-gain circuit (AGC) whose job is to keep sound levels roughly constant. Most voice recorders have AGC and it usually cannot be switched off. Last thing you need is to have your voice recorder fading in and out when picking up sound especially when the sound is at a frequency below 60 Hz between 1-4 kHz region of a wideband spectrogram of the audio range.

Revised: We have seen acoustical responses from EVP to disembodied voices recorded with a change in amplitude. We know other groups that picked up electromagnetic frequencies with devices that use a coil or modified inductive probe and has had success recording EVP. Knowing that both microphones, as well as coils are vulnerable to RF contamination, the inductive probe was designed for that purpose to sound out shielded telecommunication, and Ethernet cabling the overall burden of proof hinges on the response seeing there is no way to analyze directly the output of the inductive probe.

Altering low frequency responses (Electronic Voice Phenomena) by simply changing the pitch of any noise by slowing it down, or speeding it up can be manipulated to come up with whatever you might think it said, or want it to say. The idea is to control your environment, tag your audio; backing up your audio with video can help validate responses, use audio spectrum analysis to rule out questionable sounds that could be mistaken for evidence. The more control you have over the environment the less time is spent on audio analysis. Software like Adobe Audition will allow you to remove noise from around the sound you want to bring out. If the EVP is intended to be used as evidence, and it is not clear enough to stand on its own. Throw it out!

Electromagnetic Field Theory: (EMF) is a force given off by electric charges the force is evident in nearly everything in nature. Both living and non-living or inanimate devices emit an electromagnetic field. The higher the spikes in the electromagnetic field, the more potential there is for paranormal activity. The theory is that a ghost or spirit gives off an electromagnetic field, which can be detected by Electromagnetic Field meters. A paranormal occurrence or ghost may give off milligauss readings in the range of 1.5 mG to about 6mg, depending on the EMF meter you use. If you get a paranormal reading, the reading should not be a steady. Steady/constant readings are usually artificially created. You may have to move around to see where the reading or ghost may be taking you.

Human beings **do not** produce an alternating electromagnetic field. Electricians use these devices to detect bad wiring, and that goes for all EMF meters. The wiring in your home is alternating current AC that is manmade making your common EMF meter useless for detecting anything like a ghost. Since we do not know what a ghost is. Use of an EMF meter would suggest that a ghost could be measured. Which to date no one has. We cannot assume that anyone has it right in this field. Because as soon as they hold up one of those devices that does nothing at all they lose all credibility. They only use these devices because they saw it on a Para-non-reality TV show.

SHARED CONSCIOUSNESS

By Edward Krietemeyer

For the entity as described in Conscious Energy to exist, it would have to be reduced to a kind of parasite, feeding off our life force and even sharing our physical experiences. In some cases, this becomes a symbiotic relationship and, in other cases, individuals may experience negative reactions such as physical weakness, dominating and violent outbursts, prolonged illnesses, and wild mood swings, resulting in psychosis. This psychosis may be shared by anyone in the room, as the entity attaches itself to any vulnerable human host. The shared consciousness with a weakened human host can cause the dominating consciousness of the entity to force control over the behavior and physical being. This is generally misinterpreted as a possession. In a symbiotic connection with both human consciousness and conscious energy, the human and entity co-exist, allowing the individual to tap into a type of shared consciousness, giving them psychic abilities, also known as second sight.

In one case, I met with a woman that had proven psychic abilities since birth. She showed me a photograph taken by a method called Kirlian electro-photography, which uses an instrument with a high voltage glass electrode to create a pulsed electrical field around the human participant. Some people claim that this is a photograph of the human aura. I believe the generally accepted consensus, that the high voltage effects the film, causing the glow or corona effect. Viewing an image produced by this method, I noticed something unusual in one particular photograph. What is normally seen in these electro-photonic images is a variation in the colorful glow surrounding and enveloping the participants, but in this case, one of the images showed three anomalies that were attached around her head. The psychic claimed to have spirit guides that remained with her always and spoke to her. To me, this appeared as if the entities that had attached to her since birth had formed a symbiotic bond that linked her consciousness to the entities' conscious energy, thus allowing her the ability to connect to other conscious beings.

Revised: Some of the other oddities you will find only in the paranormal field are; you cannot throw a rock without hitting a sensitive? There are men that are self-proclaimed sensitives although I have only met one. The vast majority of the sensitives are women. I thought it might be because women have maternal instincts, but when asked I was corrected that it was an entirely different thing. Referring to some description somewhere? Everyone as a certain level of intuition, some people are more intuitive than others are. All this really means is that some people have learned to use their experiences to quickly arrive at a course of action. Testing by the James Randi educational institute shows that most claims of psychic or medium abilities are unsubstantiated. There is a long-standing one million dollar prize for proving any psychic ability.

Psychics can get away with charging people because of their disclaimer, but what about the people that make those overpriced Ghost hunting devices even though there is absolutely no proof those devices do anything to communicate, or detect Ghosts at all? How can they sell Ghost equipment when there is no proof that Ghost exists? Well they get away with it the exact same way the psychics do. Either printed on the device itself, or written into the documentation, **for entertainment purposes only!**

Most alleged ghost sightings are from people suffering from mental illnesses, parasomnia, fantasy prone personalities, and hallucinations do to medications. In other words explainable activity when you have exhausted everything only then can it be call paranormal. This is the reason why serous research teams do not use psychics, mediums, or sencitives. Activity that is not backed up by video or audio is called a personal experience, not evidence.

Diopter & Dark Sensitivity - Revised
By Edward Krietemeyer

Why did the CCTV Security camera picked up a full-bodied apparition that walked right past, and in front of the Paranormal Investigator. Why did the camera see it, and the investigator didn't?

The amount of light needed for the human eye to sense movement is much higher than the CCTV camera used which only needed a change of 6 diopters. For the human eye to sense movement, it needs two rods in the fovea working together, both needing a change of 10 diopters to sense movement. The rods are responsible for night vision, our most sensitive motion detection, and our peripheral vision.

The Human eye optimum dark-adapted vision is obtained only after a considerable period in darkness about 30 minutes. The light response of the rods peaks sharply in the blue; they respond very little to red light. It would be undesirable to examine anything with white light even for a moment. Since the rods do not respond to red, the eye can gain full dark-adapted vision. This phenomena arise from the nature of the rod-dominated dark-adapted vision, called Scotopic vision, and this is the reason why we carry flashlights that are both white, and red light capable.

Thought Energy – Revised
By Edward Krietemeyer

There is the question of why an apparition is described wearing clothing? The apparition is nothing more than mind a conscious form of energy, our physical self-decays. The once living human being has been reduced to its last cognitive state. The entity projects an image of how it last perceived itself at the point of death. Throughout our day, all short-term memory is processed as long-term physical memory. As we sleep our brain cycles through memories, reorganizing connections while strengthening proven connections between brain cells, and our synapses. We wake up feeling refreshed, and restored ready to begin the day. Our conscious self-starts over. We make new choices; what to wear, what to do, with whom we will interact, and then consciously, and subconsciously, we organize our daily routine. Each day we start with a fresh perception of ourselves: how we look, what we wear, where we go. If you were nothing more than the sum of your experiences of the last day you lived, then you would project an image of how you last perceived yourself. This is why apparitions are depicted as having a human shape. We view ourselves as having a head, arms, and legs, and even visualize the clothes we last wore. As our presence disrupts the atmosphere surrounding our conscious self, we project the image as we last viewed ourselves.

Fear Cage Theory

This is a confined or localized area with unhealthily high levels of electromagnetic radiation due to the presence of a large amount of electrical devices, unshielded electrical cables, or power junctions. Individuals with sensitivity to Electromagnetic Fields (EMF) can experience sensations of anxiety, paranoia, or nausea after prolonged exposure to these places. Some also report feelings of "being watched." The effect often gives rise to sincere but unsubstantiated claims of hauntings.
Thoughts: This is a real and valid health concern for people with low sensitivity to high EMF.

Fun House Effect

A room, or hallway, which has some structural anomaly, which the observer unconsciously recognizes as "off," resulting in subtle to extreme physical or mental discomfort. Examples include rooms with significantly out-of-square angles, hallways of unusually long and narrow length, stairs that slant or vary in size/pitch, etc. As with the "fear cage," the "fun house effect" may give rise to sincere but unsubstantiated claims of haunting.

Thoughts: This is a real and valid health concern for people with low sensitivity to high EMF.

Electromagnetic Field Theory: (EMF) is a force given off by electric charges the force is evident in nearly everything in nature. Both living and non-living or inanimate devices emit an electromagnetic field. The higher the spikes in the electromagnetic field, the more potential there is for paranormal activity. The theory is that a ghost or spirit gives off an electromagnetic field, which can be detected by Electro-Magnetic Field meters. A paranormal occurrence or ghost may give off milligauss readings in the range of 1.5 mG to about 6mg, depending on the EMF meter you use. If you get a paranormal reading, the reading should not be a steady.

Steady/constant readings are usually artificially created.

Revised Thoughts: All EMF except for a few are calibrated for alternating current AC, which is manmade, there is no proof ghost emit EM fields therefore these devices are useless for detecting ghosts.

Quartz Theory: It is believed that Quartz and/or Limestone can store energy like a crude recording device. Powerful events in history can be replayed repeatedly, and this is commonly accepted as a cause of residual hauntings.
Revised: We have found this to be true limestone is generally found in wall plaster up to the mid twentieth century

Infrared Light Theory: Many paranormal investigators believe that ghosts can be seen in the infrared light spectrum. The light we see is known as white light. Infrared light is invisible to the human eye. Sony cameras and camcorders equipped with "night shot" and using an infrared filter allow us to take footage in the daylight hours in the red light spectrum. The infrared filter blocks out 99.9% of the sun's ultraviolent rays, leaving only the IR light spectrum to be observed.
Revised: Infrared is great in no power locations but using more infrared does not increase the visibility of ghosts. Although there has been research into the ultraviolent, that has yielded results.

Universal Consciousness Theory: It is believed that spirits know what language you speak and translate their voices for you to understand.

Thoughts: It might work on TV shows but not in real life. It has been my experience that if the entity does not know the language during life they do not know it in death.

Full Moon Theory: (Full Moons, Thunderstorms, Solar Flares) the phases of the moon have an effect on the geomagnetic field. Most paranormal investigators believe that the geomagnetic fields are strongest at the full moon and the new moon phases, causing paranormal activity to intensify. Under theory, the best time to conduct an investigation is two to three days prior to a full or new moon or two to three days after a full or new moon. It is believed that ghosts draw their energy through electrical resources. If you have ever been on an investigation before and all your equipment's batteries drained down to nothing that would fall under this theory. During solar x-rays and geomagnetic storms, the air is filled with electricity from which spirits draw energy.

Thoughts: no such luck, but I have had paid venues charge more for full moon dates while I have observed no difference.

Poltergeist Theory: (Recurrent Spontaneous Psychokinesis) this theory states that psychokinetic energy may unconsciously leave the body of an emotionally charged person, usually an adolescent, and spontaneously does damage
.

Thoughts: To date there is no proof of Psychokinetic abilities. If there was the James Randi, educational institute is offering one million dollars for proof.

Soul Theory: Man was created in GOD's image, and was given an immortal soul. The soul is thought to be the eternal part of a living human being, commonly held to be separate from the body. Philosophical and religious beliefs teach that the soul is often believed to exit the body to live on after a person's death.

Thoughts: To date there is no proof that a soul, heaven, or hell exists. I will keep you advised if that changes.

Strobe Theory: With the use of Infrared (IR), and or Ultraviolet (UV), or commonly used (Standard Light). A strobe slows down this rate of speed of an object so it can be easily capture by Photographic, and or Video equipment of reported cases of shadow people, and other spirit activity that can move very fast. Now with the use of a strobe such paranormal activity can be easily captured.

Revised: The effects from the use of a strobe are well known for freezing moving objects. This can also be accomplished with editing software.

ORB Theory is not paranormal or supernatural. Research has shown that ORBs are optical anomalies caused by fine particles of matter DUST passing near the lens that is aluminate by the flash. **(Particles include dust, pollen, water particles, and insects.)** You can easily explain away camera anomalies when it comes to using or not using a flash! The new digital cameras and their compact size mean that the flash is closer to the lens illuminating every particle moving past the lens.

I have heard every type of explanation of why their ORBs are real spirit ORBs because:

It glowed: Is there a light source, any light source?

It manifested then vanished: the particle merely moved in, and out of the light source.

If you look closely, the spirit ORB has a face in it: **Pareidolia: being perceived as significant. Apophenia: the experience of seeing meaningful patterns or connections in random or meaningless data.**

The below paragraph can help explain the majority of ORBs. The rest are reflections, lens flairs, bugs, and lighting. So if you are ORB changes direction, or in one picture but not the others? This is why.

The air in any room even if the room is sealed is moving. You do not need an open window to have airflow. Simply put; particles move around in static charged clusters of particulate matter be it dust, moisture, plant pollen, and spores. One other point I wanted to make about spores, and other particulates is that lighting conditions effect the color, so each person has a different perception of what that color is. Temperature changes create convection currents that continuously circulate the air in every room. Hot air rises, and cold air falls, but there is more to this story. The hot air molecules, as they rise pushes against other air molecules that move out of the way causing some air molecules to cool, or heat up depending on walls, windows, and other surfaces. This causes continuous changing currents of air.

The majority of ORBs are DUST!

The nearest thing to a human Spirit in a ORB, are the dead skin cells that came from you, and everyone else that had passed through the room that makes up DUST...

Telepathy Theory: A popular belief is that ghost may be able to communicate through telepathy, It has been suggested ghost prefer to communicate this way for it is easier for them. Spirits might have an easier time communicating with us when we are in an unconscious state such as REM sleep and be able to communicate and manifest itself to us. Ghost might be able to produce an image of themselves in our mind's eye to use as an aid in communicating with us that our senses fall for and mistake for physical reality. If true, it would mean that an apparent hallucination or a walking dream could still be an authentic attempt at communication from the other side. In addition it would also explain why some ghost appear so substantive, even to the point where they can be touched and conversed with and why they can appear to one person in a group and not be seen by the others. This idea might also go far in explaining those meaningful a timely dreams we sometimes experience that seem to affect our life in a significant way. Of course, ghostly telepathy does not explain why we sometimes can catch a spirit on film or detected by instruments, nor does it explain how a ghost could manifest itself to two or more people at once. All tough it does appeal to the paranormal investigator in that it does explain some especially credible encounters for which there exists no physical evidence, as we; as opens another door by which a disembodied consciousness might be able to interact with its loved ones without manifesting itself. Although such a possibility could have a darker implications as well. Telepathy would go far in explaining alien abductions as well as its forerunner attacks capon woman by a nighttime apparition known as succubus that was commonly reported in Victorian times. However if ghost do communicate with us this way why do they not interact with us more often and further why don't they appear regularly to everyone. We all sleep, we all dream, we all lost loved ones we might desire to keep in touch with. So then why is not reported more than it is?

Ionized Atmosphere Theory: Spirits draw energy from the air as well as electrical devices, electrical storms, thermal energy from animals and people. Using Ionizers would increase the amount of energy aids in spirit manifestation.

Thoughts: There was a theory put forth in a paranormal TV show that may have originated elsewhere that paranormal activity increased during electrical storms. My experience is that it is good at clearing the dust from the air and reduces, along with a lens hood the likely hood of capturing Dust-Orbs in your photographs.

PARANORMAL HOBBYIST

Hobby Paranormal Groups

If you are just curious about things that go bump in the night. There are many local paranormal groups known as meet-up groups you can find online at **meetup.com** or facebook. These groups usually allow guests to sit in on group discussions. It is a good way to learn, and notice general ideas, but I would take anything you hear with a lot of healthy skepticism. The important part is learning to edit your audio; EVPs are the most common type of paranormal activity at any active location. The most the meet-up groups will do is walk through cemeteries, attend paranormal conventions, and investigate that local paid haunt. If ghost stories are your passion, and you are not looking for anything more than those weekend walks through the cemetery. Then a meet-up group is for you.

Then again if you are having trouble believing that you can communicate with the dead through a cell phone application, Ouija board, dousing rods, radio hacks, or bad photography. There are smaller very scientific based groups that are serious about what is considered evidence. They are very selective about who joins because of their focus on explaining phenomena, and uncovering the truth. To understand the science behind frequency analysis can identify the differences between noise, contamination, and a real EVP. Unlike what you would hear from most of the meet-up groups, the golden rule is; not everything is paranormal, and not every location is haunted. Real paranormal activity is very rare. Not even the most seasoned researcher has ever seen a full-bodied apparition. The more dedicated the group the more work that is expected and the greater the reward. What would be that experience of a lifetime? Being a witness to residual occurrences or maybe participating in real time communication through advanced electronic methods. Experiments are a big part of research delving into the entities cognitive abilities, dimensional state of being, and Electromagnetic Voice Research. Of course, to uncover the truth in any field you need to put in the work, and that is the difference between wanting reality, and settling for fantasy.

COMMONLY MISTAKEN FOR GHOSTS

The First most commonly reported cases of paranormal occurrences have to do with "Sleep Disorders". A Mental Phenomenon occurs at our threshold of consciousness that is a natural bodily process as we sleep, called REM atonia that results in a paralytic paralysis that prevents us from acting out in our dreams. In some instances, caught in between a sleeping and wakening state. You are aware of the paralysis, which usually passes in a few minutes as you return to full wakefulness in some cases can include visual hallucinations, or strange sensations, such as feeling a distinct foreign presence in the room, seeing shadows, or hearing footsteps. Typically, episodes would occur from a nocturnal awakening, and could happen at any time of the night. Initially, symptoms would occur at random, from weekly, to a month or two apart for the preceding month, events can increase to several times a night. People often report encountering apparition-like entities or other worldly beings including monsters popularly known as "waking dreams" or "night terrors, and has been proposed as an explanation for reports of paranormal activity.

People suffering from Schizophrenia have symptoms ranging from distorted thoughts, feelings of paranoia and hallucinations. They are usually withdrawn or easily agitated, and account for the second most commonly reported cases of paranormal occurrences. Medications can also cause similar symptoms as Schizophrenia make sure the individual that is experiencing unexplained phenomenon checks their prescriptions with a health care professional.

Fantasy prone personalities are the cause of the third most reported type of paranormal activity. A fantasy prone person is reported to spend a large portion of his or her time fantasizing, have vividly intense fantasies, have paranormal experiences, and often confuse or mix their fantasies with their real memories.

When encountering someone that is experiencing numerous hallucinations. It is always a good idea to have them consult with their doctor to check for health problems, which could be related to what they are experiencing.

EXPOSURE TO TOXINS

Carbon monoxide is odorless, colorless, tasteless, and initially a non-irritating toxic gas. Because it is very difficult for people to detect, (CO) can kill you before you are aware it is in your home, and is often mistaken for the flu. These symptoms include headaches, dizziness, disorientation, nausea, and fatigue. Carbon monoxide poisoning can become life threatening in a matter of hours. Testing for Carbon monoxide is critical with the onset of these symptoms.

Long-term exposure to high electromagnetic fields - EMF can cause serious health concerns. Devices that produce high levels of EMF will continue to emit EMFs even when turned off. Household wiring is another source of high EMF exposure; you should hire a qualified electrician to investigate and repair the cause. Symptoms from high EMF exposure are similar to Carbon monoxide poisoning, and can include biological stress, anxiety and depression.

Private Investigations: It is important to remember these people are "trusting you" with their homes, and businesses they expect an "answer" to what their experiencing. There is a fine line you dare not tread, and that is peoples health! Never take the place of a health care professional, or presume anything including the haunt without evidence to back it up! You do not want to end-up being the cause of pain and hardship to those very people that are seeking your help!

Basic Equipment Requirements

The most important piece of equipment you will ever need is an audio recorder. Most evidence caught is electronic voice phenomenon – EVP, so you will need good audio editing software. I think easily the best audio editor is Adobe Audition for its spectrum analysis function. Other highly recommended audio editor is Audacity for many good reasons first it is FREE, second it has spectrum analysis functionality.

Computers preferably a laptop or similar mobile device capable of editing audio at any location.

Cameras one compact camera to document the location not for evidence do to all the camera anomalies associated with flash photography, or bad

41

low light functionality. Camcorders as many as you can afford, because you never know when or where activity will occur the more tripod mounted camcorders you have at the location the most likely you will caught activity.

You will need a Mel-8704 but not for the reason you think. EMF meters detect AC that <u>manmade</u> alternating electromagnetic fields not Ghost like some people wanting you to believe. Like they want you to believe in their cell phone app, or iPAD apps. All of which have no purpose but to drain money from your wallet. The **Mel-8704** has a dual function. ONE: The real purpose to detect <u>bad wiring</u> that can make you, and one day your client sick. TWO: to check ambient room temperature to debunk your EVPs because the speed of sound is not fixed it is relevant to the density of the atmosphere. Other expensive EMF meters like the Tri-field natural will detect DC direct current that your heart and all small electronic devices use, but you already know you are alive. Remember we do not know what ghosts are, or what they are made of, or id ghosts exist at all. Especially when buying equipment that claims it can.

Background: the Mel-Meter was designed and developed by Gary Galka of DAS Distribution Inc. Gary is your typical, devoted family man, married 28 years, with wife and kids. However, an unfortunate incident occurred in 2004 when Gary lost his oldest of three daughters, Melissa. The device is named after his daughter 'Mel' and the model number is her year of birth (1987) and her year of passing (2004): "Mel-8704"

Flack lights with red and bright light capability. The Human eye optimum dark-adapted vision is obtained only after a considerable period in darkness about 30 minutes. The light response of the rods peaks sharply in the blue; they respond very little to red light. It would be undesirable to examine anything with white light even for a moment. Since the rods do not respond to red, the eye can gain full dark-adapted vision. This phenomena arise from the nature of the rod-dominated dark-adapted vision, called Scotopic vision, and this is the reason why we carry flashlights that are both white, and red light capable.

There is not the need for anything else most equipment created for the paranormal field does nothing at all. Mystical or spiritual tools are based on fantasy, and belief systems.

LAWS YOU SHOULD KNOW

It is illegal for anyone to be in a cemetery after dark. Moreover, just because no one lives or works in a building, does not mean it is fair game for investigating. If you are caught trespassing, your respectability in the community is finished.

Cemetery LAWS

You should be aware of local ordinances to protect the public health, safety and general welfare. As well as regulations relating to the operation, control, and management of cemeteries.

The cemetery shall be open to the public during daylight hours as established and posted by The Township Board for the purposes of burials, graves visitation or historical research.

No person shall be permitted in the cemetery after dark except by written permission. This may include any permits from the county.

Any person, firm or corporation who violates any of the provisions of this Ordinance shall be guilty of a misdemeanor and shall be subject to a fine of up to $500.00 and/or imprisonment for up to 90 days in jail as may be determined by court of law. Each day that the violation continues to exist shall constitute a separate offense. Any criminal prosecutions hereunder shall not prevent civil proceedings for abatement and termination of the activity complained of.

Trespassing LAWS

A person is guilty of criminal trespass if, under circumstances not amounting to burglary as defined:

The person enters or remains unlawfully on property; intends to cause annoyance or injury to any person or damage to any property, including the use of graffiti; intends to commit any crime, other than theft or a felony; or is reckless as to whether his presence will cause fear for the safety of another.

Is a class B misdemeanor unless it was committed in a dwelling, in which event it is a class A misdemeanor fine of up to $5,000, or imprisonment up to 7 years, or both for each violation.

Please check local ordinances for fines, and imprisonment for your county.

Remember local law enforcement and the **NSA** pays close attention to social media like facebook. Unless you do not mine being questioned, arrested or find for violating the law. Then I would not post such criminal activity.

The hobbyist should avoid clients and private property you can face legal, moral, and safety issues. You can also be held libel for all vandalism, theft, and damages. If all you want to do is go ghost hunting then paid venues abound and most of them have been featured on popular Para-non-reality TV shows. Leave those demons at home in your closet where they belong, or take the team out for movie night where monsters can frighten the bravest of you. It is better than being sued when you frighten the homeowner out of their house with talk of evil spirits, and cleansings.

The legalities does not end there is you are the founder of the team the felonies starts with you. You are responsible for anyone acting with or without your permission. The law will say that the member or members of your organization was acting on your behalf weather you knew it or not unless you have signed rules, and releases from each member that clearly states that you must have written permission obtained from the people named, and limit those names to the people you trust.

Types of documentation you should have can be found online:

- Membership Documents
- Confidentiality Agreement
- Liability Waiver
- Emergency Contact Information
- Minimum Equipment Requirements
- Membership Requirements
- Release of Likeness
- Waiver of Liability

If you intend to investigate private residences then I would strongly suggest you wait until you have gained a couple years' experience. You should at least conduct some training investigations with friends, or family, so that can review your performance before taking on private cases. Remember finishing the case with a timely reveal is the most important part.

The other documentation you will need is client release of liability:

- Client Documents
- Letter of Interest
- Permission to Investigate
- Initial Contact Report (Phone Interview 1)
- Client (Onsite Interview 2) Questionnaire
- Release of Likeness
- *Confidentiality Agreement
- Liability Waiver
- Thank You Letter

Remember to give them copies. In the 'Confidentiality Agreement', there should be previsions for data collected. Making sure that the client's privacy is safeguarded, but all evidence should belong to you. If you capture incredible data, you should have full rights over it. This is the cost of being FREE of charge.

EVP Procedure

Remember the EVP rule is pause between each question for 15 seconds, and accompanying researchers must observe total silence. The only exception is tagging unavoidable noise. Take turns do not talk over each other's EVP and practice relaxed breathing if you are a heavy breather hold your breath during the 15 seconds pauses. Drink plenty of water to keep stomach noises from occurring.

✓ Take your EM reading as soon as you enter the area looking for high EM fields that can cause illness.
✓ Speak at a consistent and moderate tone of voice 50 to 60 dB (No whispering)
✓ Avoid making any noises during the sessions (tag any noises that you are responsible for, or any other unavoidable noises, or contamination.)
✓ Keep questions short and to the point.
✓ Keep language within the period, and history of the location.
✓ Stay away from YES/NO questions.

The questions attempt to encourage the entity into giving you useable information.
Try asking them to tell you about their lives.
Ask questions that would interest you, or encourage you to answer.

Start each EVP session with {number} the time is {time} {location} {area}

NOTE: take temperatures during session.

Each accompanying researcher must state his or her {name}. (Used as a voice record for debunking)

Introduce yourself

My name is {...} I am your friend. I am here to talk to you.

Can you approach me; get as close as you can to me, and talk as loud as you can into this 'tool' it can hear your voice. (We found playing the friend card worked)

This tool cannot harm you in any way; it is the means to communicate with you. We always use the word tool because it is easily recognizable in any era, unlike device, or voice recorder.

Have as much history on the location and have already compiled a list of questions.

If you inadvertently ask YES/NO, question. Just follow it up with a WHEN HOW WHAT WHY and WHERE.

Animal in the Paranormal (Sensitivity to the Paranormal)

Dogs are trained to use the animals since of smell to detect contraband such as drugs, or bombs. To attack and defend in law enforcement, or the military, but hunt for Ghosts? There have been claims that animals can sense activity associated with Ghost. The research I have done on our common household pets and their sensitivity to their surroundings. Let us start with vision, dogs are dichromats, and have color vision equivalent to red-green color blindness. Dogs have very large pupils, a high density of rods in the fovea, an increased flicker rate, and a tapetum lucidum an adaptation toward superior night vision. Dogs can detect a change in movement that exists in a single diopter of space within their eye. (Humans require a change of between 10-20 diopters.)

Comparatively dogs can detect movement that is up to 20 times subtler than human vision. The frequency range of dog hearing is approximately 40 Hz to 60,000 Hz, which means that dogs can detect sounds far beyond the upper limit of the human auditory spectrum. Additionally, dogs have ear mobility giving them the ability to pinpoint the exact location of a sound. Eighteen or more muscles can tilt, rotate, raise, or lower a dog's ear. A dog can identify a sound's location much faster than a human can, as well as hear sounds at four times the distance. Therefore, in conclusion man's best friend your household pet would be more likely to sense the presence of a small animal in the walls, or react to noises from outside passing cars or from other dogs. Some dogs barks almost nonstop when there is no apparent season. Who is to say what they are reacting to when there are numerous of more likely explanations than a Ghost? I have heard of paranormal groups training their dog to sense EMF. We already know that inundated with electromagnetic fields. All I can see are dogs running around with their owners while playing get the Ghost as easily as get the Frisbee or the ball. Theoretically, if there were Ghost the dog has far greater sense of sight, smell, and hearing to detect subtle changes in the room without the human owner sensing anything, but therein lies the problem. We would have no idea what the dog was reacting too. How can you train a dog to react to what we, as humans have yet to prove even exists?

Different Types of Ghosts
There are other types of haunts these are the most common.

Intelligent Haunts are entities that has a very strong cognition testing has shown that they are able to read, see colors respond in full sentences shows emotion, and can move and throw objects, as well as hit, and push. The whole scratching thing is mostly from TV, even though people scratch themselves all the time. Most people believe in demonic spirit, but besides TV, and horror movies the nearest thing has been the occasional entity that we have pissed off. There are all kinds of mentality just like there are in the living. Some entities are confused not knowing that they are dead, others know that there dead and will tell you how. There has been entity that apologized for scaring us, and then others that want you dead, or will tell you they want to kill you. I have yet had anything follow me home, or harm me in any serious manner.

Residual Haunts are recurring activity without cognition. This is the type of haunt where the activity is repeated repeatedly and the imprinter died, and the activity continued. Alternatively, a traumatic event had occurred where the energy plays out repeatedly. You are not looking for a ghost, and no one needs to die. The event will keep repeating itself at the same time that it occurred every day. In 1974, there was a house fire where the house burned to the ground at 11:30 every morning the event plays over, and over again no one died in this haunt.

Help Me Help Me Daddy
Warning disturbing content: http://snd.sc/11HUuAI

Imprinting is a method to link the spirit of a once living human being to a personal object, and is another way the entity can preserve the consciousness in the haunt by imprinting to the property.

Doppelganger (German: "double goer") German folklore, a wraith or apparition of a living person, as distinguished from a ghost. The word is also used to describe the sensation of having glimpsed oneself in peripheral vision, in a position where there is no chance that it could have been a reflection. They are generally regarded as harbingers of bad luck. In some traditions, a doppelgänger seen by a person's friends or relatives portends illness or danger, while seeing one's own doppelgänger is an omen of death.

Thoughts: Although you would think this type of haunt would be less common since it is listed as folklore, but over the past eight years, we had two occurrences associated with this type of haunt.

Invisibles are ghosts that play with children that only the child can see. Some people believe these ghosts are only a figment of the child's imagination. However, others believe that children have a kind of inherent power to see ghosts, which eventually the onset of maturity stops.

Thoughts: Evidence of the ghosts of children playing with living children has been caught on camera. Just because it is a child do not dismiss it as an over active imagination.

There are many other reasons for haunts that have to do with mental disorders, sleep paralysis, anxiety disorders, or medications. Just because there is, a claim of a haunt does not mean there is one. Never assume it is haunted until reviewing all the evidence ruling out everything that is explainable first.

How to rid yourself f of a haunt

The tried and true methods have always consisted of some sort of religious ritual such as a blessing, cleansing, or exorcism. None of these methods seems to work very well, especially if the home once belonged to the entity you are seeking to banish. I picture this as similar to strangers walking into your home and beginning to paint your walls and throw out your stuff. The entity in most cases does not even know its dead, and firmly believes the house is his or hers. Splashing water around the house and telling it to leave is only going to piss it off. It would be wise to attempt to discover if it is an Intelligent Haunt, a form of Conscious Energy, or a Residual Haunt a looping pattern of energy. If it is an Intelligent Haunt and you can communicate with it, try working out a co-existence by setting ground rules.

Thoughts: Ending the haunt may not be possible! We have tried blessings cleansings from Christian to pagan beliefs we even tried a low power Electromagnetic Pulse EMP, enhancing the ground. We even set up EMF inhibitors marketed as EMF Protection. It is a device that plugs into a wall outlet, enhancing the ground, and dissipating the electromagnetic field in that location. We thought it would setup barriers preventing activity in specific areas. That did not work either eventually we can to two possible solutions. Ignoring the haunt, demanding the entity leave, or treating the entity as an unwelcome guest. No one can guarantee that they can rid the location of the haunt. Some haunt are not ghosts at all, but mental illness, common sleep normality's, or hallucinations caused by medications. Understanding that by charging for services caused by illness, or the side effects of their medications is paramount to taking advantage of the people you are intended to help.

Imagining a path to immortality

Once your consciousness has adapted to surviving outside of its human host, you might imagine that an infinite existence awaits you. However, this is, by no means, the path to immortality. Over time, the magnetic pattern that is your consciousness will fade, or become corrupted by the very environment in which you exist. Since the pattern of your consciousness was created at the point of death, all you are or will ever be is contained in that pattern. Your existence is frozen in time. Regardless of how many decades pass, you will always exist in the era in which you lived.

Team Conduct

Any conclusion without supporting evidence is baseless, and never given to the client. We should always conduct ourselves as professionals exhibiting a courteous, conscientious, and generally businesslike manner at all times. Remember the client is always watching.

Never draw any conclusions to what you may have experienced during, or after the investigation to the client. (If the client asks what we have found tell them we will need to review all the audio and video over the next three weeks. Then we will review the evidence with them in person, and try to answer all their questions.) Anything you may have thought, felt, or saw is irrelevant without evidence to back it up, and comes down to a personal experience.

Watch what you say at all times! The client is always listening! What overheard, even in idle conversation can be misunderstood. During intentional conversation, you must be clear! Everything explained to them during the reveal process. The client will have an opportunity to ask any questions they might have about the data at that time.

PARANORMAL UNITY

On social media in the paranormal field skepticism, only function is to ridicule and demean others as a type of sport known as trolling. As are some of the worst, virtues of humanity are committed under the disguise of unity.

The propaganda of Paranormal Unity is commonly used throughout the paranormal field. It has become the vehicle of choice by frauds, and bogus teams that only want to swindle, or promote their questionable evidence in the attempt to gain notoriety or fame. Originally, it was to share ideas, methods, and promote mutual respect throughout the paranormal community in the quest for the truth. The truth ended up with people using other team's ideas, and even their evidence to promote themselves. Unfortunately, I have seen groups use the excuse of Para-unity to spy on other teams, or to spread disinformation about a specific group, or a specific person. Over the past seven years of running a very successful team, I have learned that the people around you are not necessarily your friends, and I have tried to keep out of all the Para-drama in this field as much as I can. The idea that any type of Para-unity would work is flawed from the beginning. There are vast differences between teams. Why would anyone think those groups with apposing ideas, methods, and beliefs would ever work. Collaboration between two teams can worked successfully, but there has to be a lot of common ground for it to work seamlessly. If you look at all the opposing belief systems, just a simplest change in ideology has turned brother against brother. Personal ideology or beliefs systems are self-serving, and counterproductive. Methods of research, preservation of the evidence, and supporting common work ethics should be everyone's goal.

Drama in any capacity should not be tolerated this is why there is no drama in the work place. It is because troublemakers are immediately removed. One person's issues cannot be allowed to disrupt the team, and like all malcontent they immediately run to another team to spread their lies. **Paranormal Drama** it is only from the very few, and the ones that deny it the most that are the biggest contributors.

What is Evidence?

Evidence, in the paranormal field is something that can provide an explanation supporting a claim or belief. We can capture unexplained activity, but the fundamental purpose for paranormal investigator is to give logical real world explanations for what is being experienced. Not to prove a location is haunted! Begin by documenting everything starting with the claims of activity, interview witnesses then schedule a meeting with the owner to walk around, and photograph the property. It is vital to create an accurate layout of the property including floor plans. Floor plans play a pivotal part in the investigation. They are used in pre-investigation briefings, equipment deployment, and most importantly can help debunk evidence. Phenomena such as touching, objects moving, disembodied voices should be documented as observations. Any observation of an unexplained nature should be reported immediately. Since you will never know when or where such phenomena will take place it is your ability to adapt, and change with the activity, and should be the foundation of any investigative strategy. Although experiencing such phenomenon without more than one witness should be considered unreliable, unless future evidence supports the claim.

Floor Plans

Floor Plans are necessary for many reasons. First, it is important to mark down all the locations of where the claims of activity occurred. This can help identify patterns that could explain the activity. Such as exposure to high EMF or the lesser known CO_2 poisoning has been known to cause allot of paranormal claims. Although CO_2 poisoning besides causing identical symptoms as exposure to high EMF will also cause sickness, and death. If the activity is focused in a particular area a floor plan would point out a location of interests.

Second, equipment deployment by strategically placing equipment from your arsenal to improve your odds of catching activity. This is critical since you never know when or where it is going to occur. It is always a good idea to have the odds in your favor. Support equipment, such as a level, simple air streamers, or a geophone placed alongside of the trigger object such as a ball for example, to debunk claims of external forces causing the event. Placing these simple tools in the room will help support your claims of catching paranormal evidence. Finally yet importantly showing equipment placement will aid in debunking activity if there's ever any question on what was caught during evidence review. This will also keep you from losing equipment when it is time to retrieve it at the end of your investigation.

Testing Equipment in the Field

Part of our methodology is to ask HOW, and WHY. There are many claims that new equipment feeds the Ghost in some mysterious way? As soon as we make contact with the entity. We isolate a new piece of equipment in this case a negative ionizer. The claims are that the negative ionizer charges the atmosphere like an electrical storm, and the entity can use that to manipulate its environment. So we asked! Does this tool (negative ionizer) in this other room helps you, or hurts you? The response we got from the entity was "IT HURTS US!"

EM Pump: The entity really did not know what to make of it? While at the investigation of the Oakland Aviation Museum activity caught on video as the entity is heard, we are not sure if it is words or breathing. We do know that a tripod mounted EM Pump was attached to the camera. Then was heard moving down stairs by a researcher who mistakenly thought someone was behind her. Again, it appears the entity did not know what to make of the EM Pump, but we are on the right track. The theory behind this is that the entity needs an EM field to do anything from communicating, to moving objects, and manifesting an image of its former self. Some researcher believe that the entity pulls energy from the human bio-electrical field that's generated by the heart, and open circuits that produce an EM field with its flow of electrons. There are different methods, some use ionizers statically charging the air or EM Pump to producing an EM field to "feed the Ghost" as it is called. I would think providing a substantial EM field for the entity to manipulate would, and has increased activity in the manner we have use it.

Oakland Aviation Museum: http://youtu.be/H14a39UQjAk

Revised: As shown in the footage linked above that the EM pump was more of a curiosity it is unknown if it worked as perceived.

The truth of it is paranormal investigations are boring.

I admit to falling asleep from time to time, and in the most haunted places. It is a sign of a real pro when you can tag your audio while sleeping. Depending on the size of the location, we rotate small teams to keep the contamination down 2 to 3 people at a time. That is it everyone else outside, but even being outside you still have to keep the noise down! Everything ends up on audio, or video people forget that. I fell asleep on the second floor in the ballroom of the Washoe Club. We had already caught activity on the third floor where I was hit! Actually, I was backhanded in the arm. There was this cool ripple in the air that looked like predator moving away, but incredibly fast.

Trigger Objects

We use trigger objects to encourage activity. Our research into the background of the entity haunting the location uncovered a sweet tooth, so we planted treats in location of the entities death. We find trigger objects to be very useful. At the Gold Hill Hotel in Gold Hill Nevada there where claims of children playing in room 12. Trigger objects of a ball, and a poker hand was set out to catch any activity. What we caught was one card moving out of a hand of cards without moving any of the other cards in the hand. This is the video footage of the activity caught in Room 12.

Room 12: http://youtu.be/gELx5EusLO4

The biggest challenge for investigators; although widely ignored are the mental disorders that account for most claims of paranormal activity. The most common are Sleep Paralysis: Awake but still asleep people often report encountering apparition-like entities or other worldly beings, Anxiety Disorders: Post-traumatic stress caused by a recent bereavement or traumatic experience, and Mental Illness: Psychotic disorders that can alter perception. I have often seen investigators prescribe metaphysical remedies in response to spiritual claims that can only end up doing more harm than good. There are unsuspected dangers when it comes to the human mind you should never take the place of a health professional. Our memories during times of grief or illness are at their strongest. A simple act can trigger memories that can take you to a time when you envision what you expect to see, even if what you are envisioning is no longer there. Then other times it is a matter of assuming or mistaken what was seen. It is normal for your brain to fabricate a mental representation for a substituted reality. How our brain deals with processes sensory input, comprises how we perceives the world around us, and a lot of the time that perception is wrong. We see the world around us as stable, even though our sensory input is incomplete, and rapidly changing.

EASY TO BUILD HOBBY STYLE PROJECTS

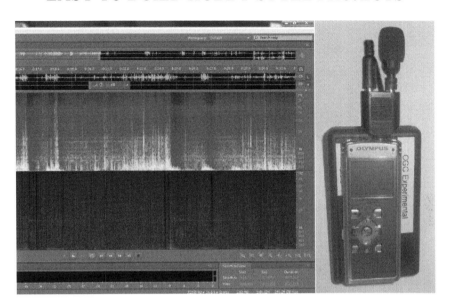

Record both EMF/Voice on your stereo audio recorder one of many ways to validate your EVPs. This is primarily used during experiments by simultaneously recording both together. You can show that your EVP is not RF contamination. What you would need is,

- Stereo Audio Recorder
- Stereo splitter
- Mono Microphone
- Mono coil Microphone: This is similar to the stereo coil microphone except mono is one channel instead of two. The stereo coil microphone will not work it needs to be split into two mono devices.

This method was devised to disprove the skeptical explanation for electronic voice phenomena EVP. That EVP are Radio Frequencies called RF contamination. This device is used to record samples electromagnetic contamination.

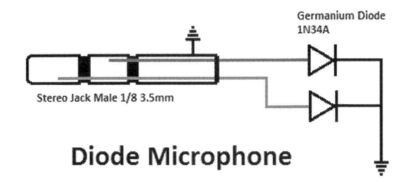

Diode Microphone

If the entity is an electromagnetic pattern of consciousness that is able to manipulate its electromagnetic properties creating what is known as an Electromagnetic Voice - emV. Then we should be able to isolate, and record the entities emV using the Raudive Diode or RF Coil microphones used in early experiments by Dr. Konstantin Raudive. These devices have been created to rule out all acoustical sources by only picking up an EM field for the purpose of recording the EM response, and then saving the acoustical sound by feeding the output of the device to a digital recorder. Of course, the world is inundated with electromagnetic frequencies from our personal smart phones to radio devices of all kinds. Who has to say if the entity uses any part of the EM field at all?

If by capturing intelligent responses from within our shielded control environment. Would we then prove the entity could manipulate its electromagnetic properties by capturing an intelligent electromagnetic response?

We setup to test these microphones at a claimed haunted location Inside the Miner's Cabin on Sept 11 and the 12th 2012 at the Gold Hill Hotel in Nevada. We will test our first of three EM field recorders, and below our feet the Yellow Jacket Mine Disaster where at least thirty-five miners died, and where some bodies were never retrieved. The fire persisted, so miners sealed off the offending levels, which remained hot for several years.

After two days of recording audio, and video the Radio Frequency - RF coil microphone picked up man made frequencies. Something we expected if it worked at all. Neither the RF coil microphone alongside three standard acoustical recorders, and three video cameras picked up any paranormal responses during our EVP sessions. Even though the location has been known for paranormal activity, and had even been on a paranormal reality TV show. This was our second investigation at that location, so without data, we have no conclusion from this experiment, but we find the RF Coil microphone more sensitive to RF contamination then the Raudive Diode. These two projects the Diode and coil microphones are very easy projects anyone can build, since these devices only pickup electromagnetic fields it would be a good way to debunk skeptical claims about electronic voice phenomenon – EVP, and for that purpose, we use them on all our investigations.

Example of RF Contamination.

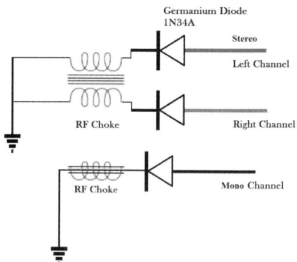

Germanium Diode
1N34A

Stereo

Left Channel

RF Choke

Right Channel

RF Choke

Mono Channel

RF Coil Microphone

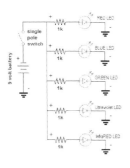

5x 10mm **LED FULL SPECTRUM**

Full Spectrum Cameras

There has been a move toward using full spectrum cameras. Somehow, paranormal groups assumed that digital cameras could not distinguish ultraviolet light from the infrared light in which paranormal activity occurs. Therefore, there are an overwhelming number of paranormal groups wanting to know how to convert the standard digital cameras to full spectrum cameras. The truth is that all digital cameras are capable of full spectrum imaging. The digital camera CMOS or CCD image sensors are also sensitive to ultraviolet light and, even more so, to infrared light. Manufacturers filter out both the UV and IR portions of the light spectrum, blocking them from ever reaching the sensor. If they allowed the visible spectrum through, this would make the images look unnatural. The conversion involves simply removing the internal filter assembly and replacing it with a clear filter that is transparent from 280nm all the way past 2000 nm - Nanometer.

Revised: Video cameras are all the same it is a good idea to replace the filter with a piece of clear photo glass if you do the modification yourself. The mods I have seen on cheap cameras really jack up the camera. One I had inspected in particular wouldn't auto focus the cameras shutter speed was set to low light, turning every bad picture that was taken in to images of ghosts! Well they wished they caught a real ghost. I have yet to see usable evidence from Full Spectrum images if only to hear some oohs and aahs! from the client. You need to use a lot of light with these cameras white light would be perfect since white light contains the full light spectrum, it's cheaper, but takes away from that all needed spooky ghost hunting feeling.

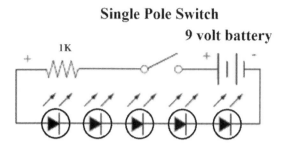

Single Pole Switch

9 volt battery

5 x 10mm Infrared LED

The 5 LED simple IR LED camera light as shown. 5 LEDs from the switch + positive to - negative, I would only use 10mm Triple Chip 200mW LEDs the single chip don't last long. The project box is from Radio Shack, so is the switch. The Vivitar Hot Shoe you can find on ebay as well as the battery holder, and 1k resistors. I would not exceed more than 5 LED in a strand. Strands 5 LED and below must have one 1k resistor the more LEDs you add in a light the need for a resistor isn't necessary. Lithium batteries last 12 hours in lights built with 5 to 12 LED; there is a way by adding a timing circuit that will extend battery life up to 5x longer by pulsing the LEDs as shown in the IC LM555 electronic schematic. All of these lights are very easy to build, and will save you hundreds of dollars on store bought, and hobby built lights.

I frosted the outer LEDs on this light to defuse the Infrared. The LEDs have a 30-degree lens that produces a focused spot of Infrared, so to defuse that spot I sanded the lens gently with fine grit sand paper. It gives a much more uniformed look to your videos. The largest light I have built was 20 Triple Chip 10mm LED that made everything looks like day.

Single Pole Switch

9 volt battery

8 x 10mm Infrared LED

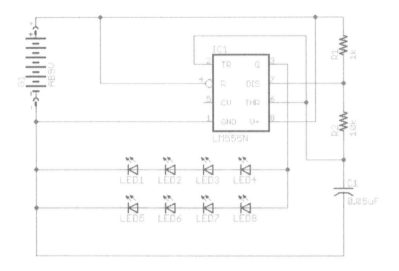

This electronic schematic, I use an IC LM555 precision timer to pulse the LEDs to extend battery life five times longer.

You may of notice as you review your video evidence that the light slowly fades out. How you fix that is by adding an IC Voltage Regulator LM7805 to the circuit between the switch, and ground. This will give you a more consistent level of light. The lithium battery will drain completely before the light goes out.

How to build Negative & Positive Static Field Detectors

I would like to thank Mike StClair of ViperRIP Paranormal with his YouTube instructional videos on building this device.

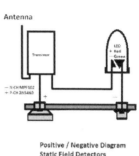

There are two types of single circuit static field detectors you can build.

MPF102 N-Channel Transistor used for the Negative detector.
2N5460 P-Channel Transistor used for the Positive detector.

These are very simple to build using a 9 volt battery, 9 volt battery snap connector, Green LED for the Negative, and Red LED for the positive depending on which field circuit your building. You must strip the plastic cover off the snap connectors to uncover the brown circuit board then cut the wires off, now you are ready to solder them together as indicated above. The transistor is always facing down round side up. The diagram to your below can be used for both N-Channel and P-Channel transistors, and are soldered into the battery snap connector. The LEFT wire is used as an antenna and is bent strait up. The MIDDLE wire is soldered into the Positive side of the Battery Snap Connector, and the RIGHT wire is soldered to the Positive side of the LED. The LED as shown to your left has to wires the Positive side is always longer. The Negative end has a flat side as shown. Solder the RIGHT wire to the Positive side of the LED, and the Negative side into the Negative side of the battery snap connector, and that is it.

One other thing I would suggest gluing the wire on the LEFT side of the transistor used as the antenna to the transistor itself. The wire is very fragile by gluing it to the side will help from breaking it off.

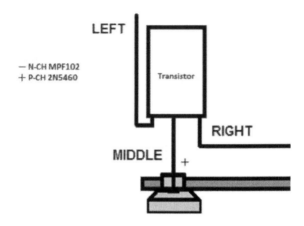

Positive Side Battery Snap Connector

Even though I really cannot see a need for this device many people are interested in building them, and it is a very simple project when starting to build and test your own equipment. The left wire is very fragile used as an antenna is very easily broken off so I built both positive and negative transistors into a project box that is shown next.

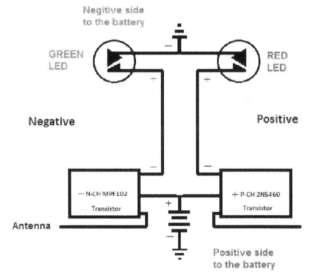

Negative / Positive Diagram
Static Field Detectors

How to build a Geophone

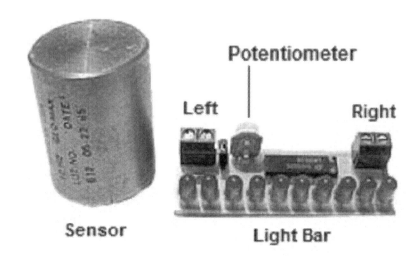

You will need to buy a Geophone Seismic Kit online, but wait until receiving it before buying the project box. The sensor is a cylinder that comes in different sizes. You will not know which size sensor they will ship with your kit until you get it. The price for these keeps going up around $30-$40 BG Micro is where I usually find the kit. Once you receive the kit, and then buy the correct size project box. The sensor shown above must mount firmly down on the base inside of the project box. Do not use glue under the base it will reduce the sensitivity of the sensor, just put glue on the sides of the cylinder. I used an aluminum project box shown above its heavier, but plastic works just fine. The light bar mounts on top; you will need to drill two holes for wiring. In image of the light bar the right side connects, the power the left side connects the sensor.

You will need to solder the wires on the sensor shown above in the top, and the images shown. The middle post usually the ground and the outer contact being the positive. This differs between manufactures of the sensor. Look for the positive side post marked as shown in the image on the next page. I believe they still provide instructions, but I would not count on it. The other parts you will need are a 9-volt battery holder, and push on/off switch you can find at Radio Shack.

It has a potentiometer the round white wheel next to the left wire connector in the above image. It is how you adjust the sensitivity of the device. The slightest touch near the device will register on the light bar. The adjustment is so when tapping near the surface registers two or three LEDs you do not need it so sensitive that it picks up every little vibration even though it is capable of doing so if needed.

I build and test my own equipment therefore; I have a better understanding on how my equipment works. I have not seen much in the way of equipment used, and designed for the paranormal field that has any proven purpose at all. Only a couple things I build that are either practical or necessary, and those are Geophones just shown, Infrared LED lights, and I have had some favorable results from an EM pump I well show you how to build.

Electromagnetic Field Generators
A couple very easy EM projects

The theory behind this is that the entity needs an EM field to do anything from communicating, to moving objects, and manifesting an image of its former self. Some researcher believe that the entity pulls energy from the human bio-electrical field that's generated by the heart, and open circuits that produce an EM field with its flow of electrons. There are different methods, some use ionizers statically charging the air or EM Pump to producing an EM field to "feed the Ghost". I would think providing a substantial EM field for the entity to manipulate would, and has increased activity in the manner we have use it. Each one of these project are easy to build costing $25 for the EM Pump and $39 for the Vortex EM Pump. Depending on how frugal you can get you can build these for half the price; it is up to you on how well you can find deals online.

The EM Pump & Vortex EM Pump

This simply is two electromagnetic fields turning into each other creating an electromagnetic funnel of sorts. Some believe that it creates an EM beacon attracting the entity. I have video evidence of something doing just that. You cannot see it, but you can definitely hear it come up to the camera I had the EM pump mounted on.

For both EM projects, you will need to glue the magnet up right to the top of the motor making it as centered as possible. This will keep the vibrations in the fan down reducing noise. Remember to eliminate as much noise as possible to keep from contaminating evidence. That is why I used the fan motors because they operate quietly. That is all you need for the EM Pump one-fan motor, one magnet. The Vortex EM Pump need two fan motors with magnets one mounted on the bottom of the project box (4x2x1) spinning left to right, one mounted on the lid on the direct opposed side hanging down with a reverse spin right to left. This will spin magnetic fields into each other creating the Vortex EM field.

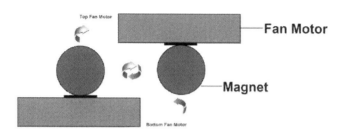

Vortex EM Pump

What you will need for the simple EM projects:

1. Single Pole Switch
2. RED LED used as a power indicator
3. 12VDC Micro Fan Model: 273-240 Catalog #: 273-240 the difference between the EM Pump, and the Vortex Pump are the number of fans. Moreover, I used this fan motor because it is quiet.
4. Round Ceramic Magnet (Rare Earth Are Better)
5. Project box I used the (3x2x1") for the EM Pump, and the (4x2x1") for the EM Vortex Pump (any other sizes can be used)
6. 9 volt battery holder

Thoughts: A vortex pump according to the originator acts like a beechen attracting ghost to it. It not like the EM pump created to feed the ghost to make it stronger although it had the same effect.

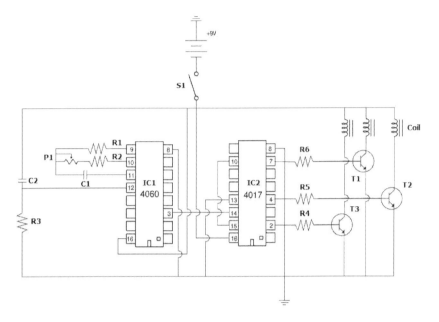

How to Make an EM Pump Electronic Circuit
Electronics Technical skills are highly recommended.

This EM Pump uses no magnets, and is harder to build, but is completely quiet. The cost is much less than the two examples above running around $20.

What you will need for the electronic EM project:

1. S1 = Single Pole Switch
2. R1 = 2M2
3. R2 = 1K
4. R3 = 1M
5. R4, R5, R6 = 220 OHMS
6. P1 = 100 POT
7. C1 = 10uF/16v non polar
8. C2 = 1uF
9. T1, T2, T3 = TIP122
10. IC1 = 4060
11. IC2 = 4017

REFERENCE

Dr. Celia Green of the Institute of Psychophysical
Research 1968
Princeton University's Engineering Anomalies Research
James Randi Foundation

The Physics of Time Travel
Theories for The Paranormal: > Time Slip Theory
Time Slips on Wikipedia
String theory Wikipedia

About.com
Paranormal Phenomena quote from Dr. Hans Holzer
Four Dimensional Being
Princeton University quote
Three-dimensional world video (YouTube)
By Dr. Michio Kaku, professor of theoretical physics at City College of
New York

Exchangeable image file format EXIF
Pareidolia quote
Ideomotor Effect quote Wikimedia

Electronics Basics: What Is Alternating Current?
By Doug Lowe from Electronics All-In-One Desk Reference for Dummies.
(Online Article)

In the Midst of Darkness: The Study of Ghosts by Edward W. Krietemeyer
The websites of CGC - Ghost Chasing Need to Know Blog
Institute Of Spectrological Research

GLOSSARY OF TERMS

A

Active: Ongoing reported claims of a haunting, or unexplained paranormal phenomenon.

Agent: A living person who is the focus of poltergeist activity.

Alien Entity: A paranormal entity that is not of earthly (i.e.: human or animal) origin.

Amulet: An object that is thought to bring good luck or have the power to protect from ghosts or spirits and ward off evil.

Anomaly: A strange occurrence that cannot be rationalized by objective, critical scientific evaluation.

Apparition: See Physical Manifestation.

Apport: A physical object that can materialize and appear at will in the presence of a medium.

Asport: A physical object that a spirit teleports to another location or makes disappear.

Astral Body: The body that a person occupies during an out-of-body experience.

Astral Plane: A world that is believed to exist above our physical world.

Astral Projection: The intentional act of having the spirit leave the body, whereas an out-of-body experience will happen involuntarily. (See out of body experience).

Astrology: The theory and practice of the positions and aspects of celestial bodies in the belief that they have an influence on the course of natural earthly occurrences and human affairs.

Aura: An invisible emanation of light that seems to surround a person or thing, which is often thought to reflect a person's personality.

Automatic Writing: This method of obtaining information from disembodied spirits is used by mediums in which the spirit takes control over the medium causing them to translate unconscious information on paper without being aware of the contents.

Automatism: An unconscious or involuntary muscular movement caused by spirits. (See automatic writing).

Autoscopy: The visual hallucination or image of one's body looking back at themselves from a position outside the body. (See out of body experience).

B

Ball Lightning: A rare form of lightning in the shape of a glowing red ball that can last anywhere from a few seconds to several minutes. Typically associated with Thunderstorms, these spheres are thought to consist of ionized gas.

Banshee: A wailing spirit or "death omen" that will appear to be in two different places at the same time.

Benevolent Entity: A supernatural being that actively works for the benefit of those around it.

Benign Entity: A supernatural entity that neither actively harms nor helps those around it.

C

Call: A call is the response that is made by a subject during a card-guessing test or during any other type of ESP test.

Card Guessing: Card guessing is used as an experimental test for ESP in which a subject tries to guess the identity of a set of cards.

Case Study: An in-depth investigation of an individual subject.

Channeling: In this modern day method of spirit communication, a spirit will pass information directly to a medium or channeler who will then relay the information on to the listener(s).

Clairaudience: A general term for clairvoyance and clairaudience. Clairsentience typically occurs in the form of ESP through physical sensations or smells.

Clairvoyance: An acute insight or perceptiveness that enables you to see objects or events that cannot be perceived by the senses in the form of mental imagery and intuition. (See ESP).

Closed Deck: A set of cards used in a card guessing deck in which each card will appear a fixed number of times. The statistical analysis obtained from a closed card deck differs from that of an open card deck. (See Card Guessing).

Cold Reading: This is a technique commonly used by fake mind readers, mediums and magicians, which allows them to obtain previously unknown information about a person by asking a general series of statements, questions and answers.

Control: This is a procedure in paranormal psychology that ensures that the experiment is conducted in a standard fashion so that the results will not be influenced by any extraneous factors.

Control Group: A group of outside subjects whose performance or abilities are compared with the experimental subjects.

Collective Apparition: A rare type of sighting in which more than one person sees the same apparition or phenomena.

Crisis Apparition: An apparition that is seen when a person is seriously ill, seriously injured or at the point of death.

Cryptid: A living non-human paranormal entity.

D
Dead Time: See Witching Hour.

Debunk Disprove a claim of paranormal phenomenon or activity. This is accomplished either by discovering its true source, or else by being able to readily recreate the phenomenon or so that doubt exists as to a paranormal source for the incident. (Ex: passing car headlights shining through house windows appear to be moving shadows or orbs.)

Dematerialization: This word is used to describe a spirit or specter meaning to deprive of or lose apparent physical substance or in simpler terms, without flesh.

Déjà vu: An impression or dull familiarity of having seen or experienced something before.

Demon: An inferior deity often spoken of in religious text as pure evil.

Direct Voice Phenomenon (DVP): An auditory "spirit" voice that is spoken directly to the sitters at a séance.

Dice Test: An experimental test in which a subject attempts to influence the fall of dice. This study is used for the investigation of Psychokinesis.

DOP: (disappearing object phenomenon) - is a relatively common phenomenon in which an object disappears from view and later inexplicably returns. For example, a person puts their car keys on a kitchen counter, where they are always kept. When the person goes to get them, they are gone. A thorough search turns up nothing. Later, the keys are found on the counter where they were originally put (or some other obvious place. It is difficult to document a genuine DOP occurrence because people can be careless, simply misplace things or be forgetful. However, there are many compelling stories from people who are certain they looked for the object in the place that it later appears. In some cases, people audibly call out for the object to be returned - and it is. In some rare cases, the missing object has actually been seen materializing out of thin air. It is also known as the "borrower" phenomenon. It may be related to poltergeist phenomena.

Doppelgänger: (German: "double goer") - An existence of a spirit double, or ghost an exact but usually invisible replica of a living person or any other sort of physical double. Seeing one's own doppelgänger is an omen of death.

E

Earthbound: A term referring to a ghost or spirit that was unable to cross over to the other side at the time of death and is therefore stuck on earth.

Ectoplasm: An immaterial or ethereal substance associated with spirit manifestations.

Electromagnetic Field: A measurable field of electrical energy. Some believe that anomalous shifts in the electromagnetic field can be evidence of a ghost attempting to manifest. Others believe that ghosts are drawn to high-level electromagnetic fields.

Electronic Voice Phenomenon (EVP): A form of Instrumental Trans-Communication wherein anomalous disembodied voices and sounds that are not immediately heard by human ears, but are picked up on recording equipment or other electronics designed to capture or transfer sound so that they can be listened to later.

Elementals: Spiritualists commonly refer to this term to describe mean or angry spirits sometimes also called "Earth Spirits".

EMF: See Electromagnetic Field.

EMF Sensitivity: A condition wherein a person or animal is sensitive to the effects of high levels of electromagnetic energy. Everyone is sensitive to these fields to a degree, though some are more so than others are. Symptoms of EMF sensitivity include nervousness, skin irritation, headache, and can even give an affected person a feeling that they are "being watched." Prolonged exposure to high-level EMFs (or short-term exposure with extreme sensitivity) can also lead to drastic mood changes and hallucinations.

EVP: See Electronic Voice Phenomenon.

Extra Sensory Perception (ESP): Communication or perception by means other than the physical senses.

Exorcism: The banishment of an entity or entities i.e. spirits, ghosts and demons that is thought to possess or haunt a location or human being or animal. An exorcist who will call upon a Higher Power to cast away any evil forces that may reside there conducts the ritual, which can be religious in nature.

F

False Awakening: The event in which a person believes they are awake but are actually dreaming.

G

Ghost: Disembodied energy that interacts with the material world in a seemingly intelligent, patterned or organized manner.

Ghost Buster: An individual who claims to be able to remove or purge a paranormal entity from a location.

Ghost Hunt: The practice of going to a place where there are not necessarily accounts of paranormal activity, and seeing if any such activity can be witnessed and/or documented.

Ghost Hunter: A person who actively seeks out paranormal entities or looks to have an experience with the paranormal.

Goat: An experiment in which the subject does not believe in the ability for which they are being tested.

Ghoul: Demonic or parasitic entity that feeds upon human remains.

H

Hallucination: The perception of sights and sounds that is not actually present.

Haunting: A state of being wherein research and evaluation cannot explain away multiple consistent anomalous occurrences and a conclusion is drawn that certain events taking place at or about the location are of paranormal origin.

Hellhound / Black Shuck: A spectral death omen in the form of a ghostly dog.

Hot Reading: A devious or fraudulent reading in which the reader has been given prior knowledge of the sitter.

Hypnosis: A technique that induces a sleep like state in which the subject acts only on external suggestion.

I

Ignis fatuus: A phosphorescent or spectral light that that is alleged to be an indication of death. This phenomenon is thought to be caused by spontaneous combustion of gases emitted by rotting organic matter.

Illusion: A delusional perception between what is perceived and what is reality.

Intuition: Non-paranormal knowledge that is gained through a perceptive insight.

Instrumental Trans-Communication: A general term used to describe the phenomena of communication with supernatural entities via electronic devices.

Intelligent Entity: A supernatural being that evidences intelligence and will of its own.

ITC: See Instrumental Trans-Communication.

Inhuman Entity: A ghost or paranormal entity that is not of earthly human origin.

L

Levitation: To lift or raise a physical object in apparent defiance of gravity.

Life Review: A flashback of a person's life that is typically associated with near-death experiences.

Lucid Dreaming: A dream state in which one is conscious enough to recognize that one is in the dream state and is then able to control dream events.

M

Magnetometer (EMF, gaussmeter): An instrument for measuring the magnitude and direction of a magnetic field typically used by paranormal researchers to detect a ghost's magnetic energy.

Malevolent Entity: A supernatural entity that actively works to harm or terrorize those around it.

Marian Apparitions: The event in which the Virgin Mary is seen.

Materialization: The act of forming something solid from the air. One of the most difficult and impressive materializations is when part or all of a ghost or spirit can be seen, especially if the face is recognizable.

Matrixing: Tendency for the human mind to interpret sensory input (that which is perceived visually, audibly or tactilely) as something familiar or more easily understood and accepted, and in effect mentally "filling in the blanks".

Medium: Someone who professes able communicate with spirits on behalf of another living being, acting as a midway point halfway between the worlds of the living and the dead.

Mesmerism: A hypnotic induction of a sleep or trance State (See Hypnotism).

Mist: A Photographed anomaly that appears as a blanket of light. There is no substantial proof that these are related to paranormal phenomenon.

Motor Automatism: Bodily movement or functions that are accompanied but not controlled by consciousness (See automatic writing).

N
Near Death Experience (NDE): An experience that is reported by people who clinically die, or come close to actual death and are revived. These events often include encounters with spirit guides, seeing dead relatives or friends, life review, out-of-body Experiences (OBE), or a moment of decision where they are able to decide or are told to turn back.

O
Old Hag Syndrome: A nocturnal phenomena that involves a feeling of immobilization, suffocation, odd smells and feelings and is sometimes accompanied my immense fear (See Sleep Paralysis).

Orb: A lighting anomaly that appears in photographs and video. Orbs are small glowing balls that hover or fly about in the air. Some believe that orbs are manifestations of spirits. Others believe that they are simply the effect of ambient energy. Most of the time, they are light reflecting off dust.

Ouija Board: A pre-printed board with letters, numerals, and words used to receive spirit communications. Typically, a planchette is employed to spell out words and point out numbers or letters.

Out-of-body experience (OBE): A sensation or experience in which ones self or spirit travels to a different location than their physical body (See Astral Projection).

P

Paranormal Entity: Any being that modern science has not officially recorded or classified.

Paranormal Investigation: The practice of going to a location where accounts of paranormal activity have been reported, and working to investigate, rationalize, and/or document those specific claims.

Paranormal Investigator: A person who investigates or researches the activity of paranormal entities.

Parapsychologist: An academically trained individual who specializes in the field of parapsychology.

Parapsychology: A branch of the academic field of psychology that deals with the study of psychic phenomena and the human mind's capabilities to directly affect the material world.

Percipient: A person who sees (i.e., perceives) an apparition.

Phantom Smell: Anomalous smells with no definable source that can be smelled by unaided normal human olfactory senses.

Phantom Sound: Anomalous sounds with no definable source that can be heard by unaided normal human auditory senses.

Phantom Touch: The anomalous sensation of being physically touched, despite no physical contact being made with a material being or object.

Photographic Manifestation: A form of Instrumental Trans-Communication wherein the image of a paranormal entity is captured on film or video, or via digital means.

Physical Manifestation: A situation wherein a supernatural entity physically appears in a manner visible to unaided normal human visual senses.

Poltergeist: a non-human spirit entity, which literally means "noisy ghost" but is usually more malicious and destructive than ghosts of dead human beings. Traditional poltergeists activities are thumping and banging, levitating or the moving of objects, stone throwing and starting fires. It is thought that an adolescent agent or females under the age of 25 may bring on poltergeist activity in some instances subconsciously.

Possession: the taking over of a person's mind and/or body by a spirit, usually demonic, against that person's will. A rare phenomenon that often mimics mental illness, true possession is nowadays recognized by many religions as uncommon but genuine. It is considered a spiritual attack that requires the help of a trained clergy or spiritual counselor to resolve by performing an exorcism. Different from a demonic haunting in that it affects a single victim at a time.

Precognition: The ability to predict or have knowledge of something in advance of its occurrence, especially by extrasensory perception (See Clairvoyance).

Psi: A letter in the Greek alphabet that denotes psychic phenomena.

Psychic: A person who is responsive to psychic forces with above average ESP abilities.

Psychokinesis (PK): The power of the mind to affect matter without physical contact, especially in inanimate and remote objects by the exercise of psychic powers.

Psychometry: The ability or art of divining information about people or events associated with an object solely by touching or being near to it.

PK Activity: See Psychokinetic Activity.

Psychokinetic Activity: The anomalous event of inanimate physical objects being moved without interacting with a material entity or other discernible mundane source that would cause movement.

Pyro-kinesis: The ability to unconsciously control and sometimes in rare cases produces fire with their mind only.

R
Radio Voice Phenomenon (RVP): Receiving the voice of a deceased human being through a regular radio.

Reciprocal Apparition: An extremely rare type of spirit phenomenon in which both the agent and percipient are able to see and respond to each other.

Residual Entity: A supernatural entity that evidences no intelligence or will of its own, and simply acts out the same scene or pattern of behavior repeatedly.

Remote Viewing: Used by some psychics, this is a procedure in which the percipient or psychic attempts to become physically aware of the experience of an agent who is at a distant, unknown location through ESP.

Retro-cognition: An experience in which a person finds himself or herself in the past and is able to see and experience events in which they had no prior knowledge.

Rod: Similar to an orb, except shaped like a straight or bent tube or line.

S
Séance: A meeting or gathering of people, usually lead by a medium to receive spiritualistic messages, manifestations or communication with the dead.

Shaman: A member of certain tribal societies who acts as a medium between the visible world and an invisible spirit world and who practices magic or sorcery for purposes of healing, divination, and control over natural events.

Sheep: An experiment in which the subject believes in the ability in which they are being tested.

Simulacra: This is a word used to describe the seeing of faces, figures and images in ordinary, everyday object such as rocks, foliage, etc.

Specter: See Ghost.

Spirit: See Ghost.

Spiritualism: The belief system that the dead are able to communicate with the living, through an intermediary or medium.

Stigmata: Unexplained bodily marks, sores, or sensations of pain corresponding in location to the crucifixion wounds of Christ.

Supernatural Entity: See Paranormal Entity.

T
Tarot Cards: A set of (usually 72) cards that include 22 cards representing virtues and vices, death etc. used by fortunetellers to help predict future events.

Telekinesis: The paranormal movement of objects by scientifically inexplicable means.

Telepathy: Communication from one mind to another through means other than the senses.

Teleportation: A method of transportation in which matter or information is dematerialized, usually instantaneously, at one point and recreated at another.

Thought Form: An apparition produced solely by the power of the human mind.

Trance: A hypnotic, cataleptic, or ecstatic state in which one becomes detached from their physical surroundings.

V

Vortex: Similar to an orb, except shaped like a triangle or cone. Some believe that these are indicators of a rift between the material and spirit world.

W

Witching Hour: It is believed that 3:00 a.m. is when demonic activity is at its strongest because it is the point of the day furthest from 3:00 p.m., the time of Christ's death. (It is a way for demons to mock the holy trinity.)

White Noise: An Acoustical or electrical noise of which the intensity is the same at all frequencies within a given band.

XYZ

Paranormal • Belief • Mind • Books • Research • Culture & Science •
Afterlife • Belief • Ghost • History • Education

18549576R00054

Printed in Great Britain
by Amazon